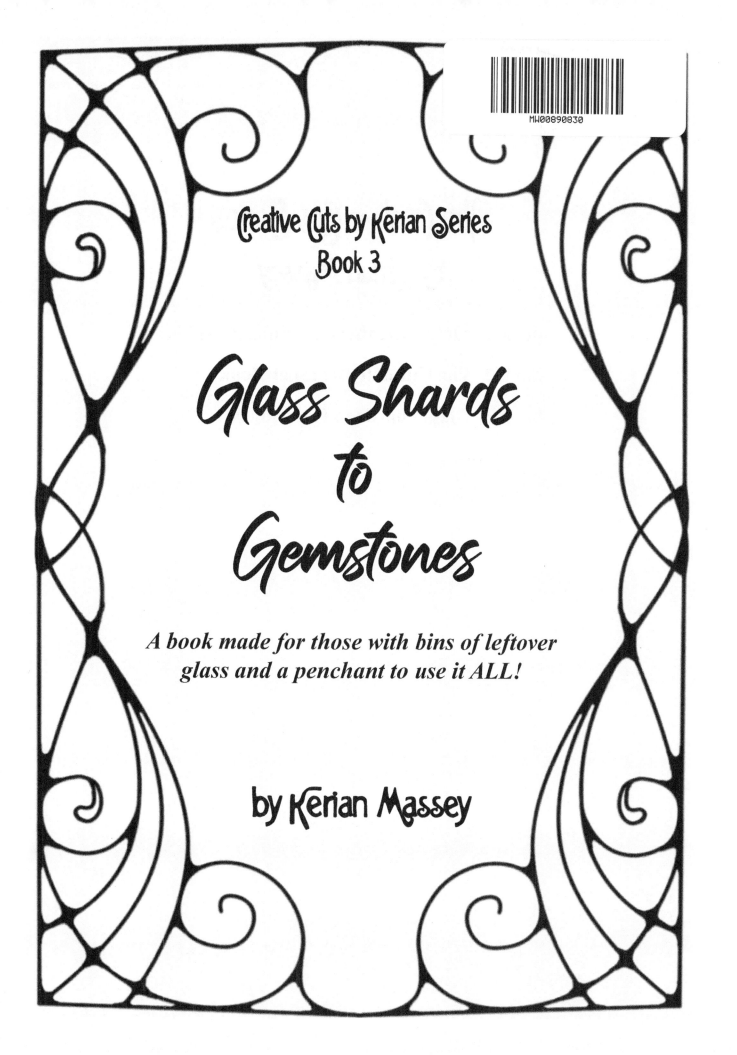

Creative Cuts by Kerian Series
Book 3

Glass Shards to Gemstones

A book made for those with bins of leftover glass and a penchant to use it ALL!

by Kerian Massey

The Creative Cuts Series
by Kerian Massey

Authors Note

To get a FREE PDF COPY of this book to use on your computer, you must email a proof of purchase of this book to creativecutsbykerian@gmail.com

Glass Shards to Gemstones

I have been trying to figure out what exactly to do with all the extra glass that one gets in the creation of a larger piece. One can only create sooo many scrappy birds before one looses their mind. In my search, I discovered these brilliant shapes, crafted by jewelers for thousands of years. I had an epiphany. Each cut is just a bunch of shards, with only 1 real substantial piece for the center! So here we are! I am not going to pretend that the cuts of stone are even remotely my design, but this idea seems pretty original to stained glass, surprisingly. So why not create a simple book that makes use of such a fun concept? Empty your bins and make really easy art. It's great becuase you have to get a bit more precise on sizes, but you don't need to use up your good glass. I have found this book to be a great learning tool for getting more precise and soldering meeting points.

Each pattern can be morphed into a unique mirror or frame. I have had someone suggest leaving the center open to hang a crystal in the middle. I love that idea and actually may try it on the piece I'm currently working on. You may even see it grace the cover as an example.Also, the more variety of a hue, the more crystal looking the design will be. So don't try to use all the same glass, nor should you since it's about using up all your leftover stuff.

Thank you so much for trying out this newest book. I hope that you enjoy it. Please keep an eye out for future books in the *Creative Cuts by Kerian* series. I'm planning on crafting a really unique Halloween book and of course a Christmas book. All will be tailored to beginner to intermediate artists. I may even throw in some multi-level designs, so you can work your way up in difficulty over time! I'd love to hear suggestions on subject matter for both! Please email **creativecutsbykerian@gmail.com** I will be happy to take both ideas and corrections.

Don't forget to share all your hard work! I definitely would love to see what you come up with from these patterns. Please post your finished stained glass pieces with the *#patternbyKerian* on your favorite social media platform. You can also follow my art page *@Keriansart* on Instagram, where I share a plethora of art projects that span a variety of mediums. It's definitely not just glass.

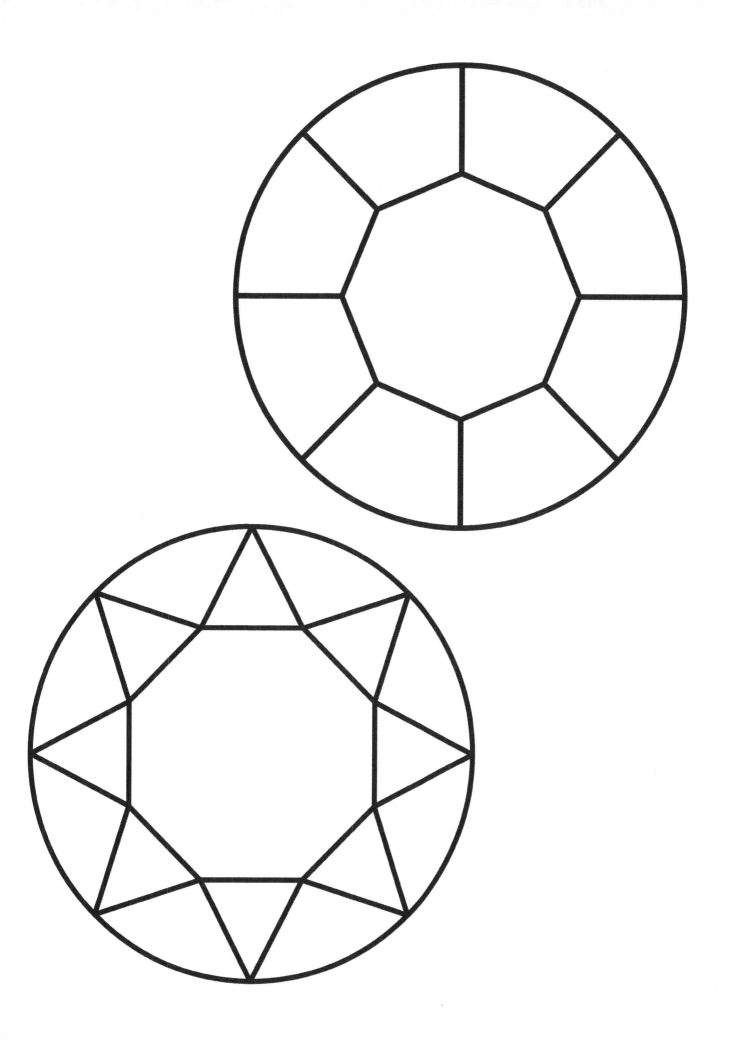

Don't forget that all of these designs can be reimagined as picture frames or mirrors! These two could be fabulous rainbow suncatchers!

*The heart style could be created without the center piece,
and then you can add a lovely crystal to hang from inside.*

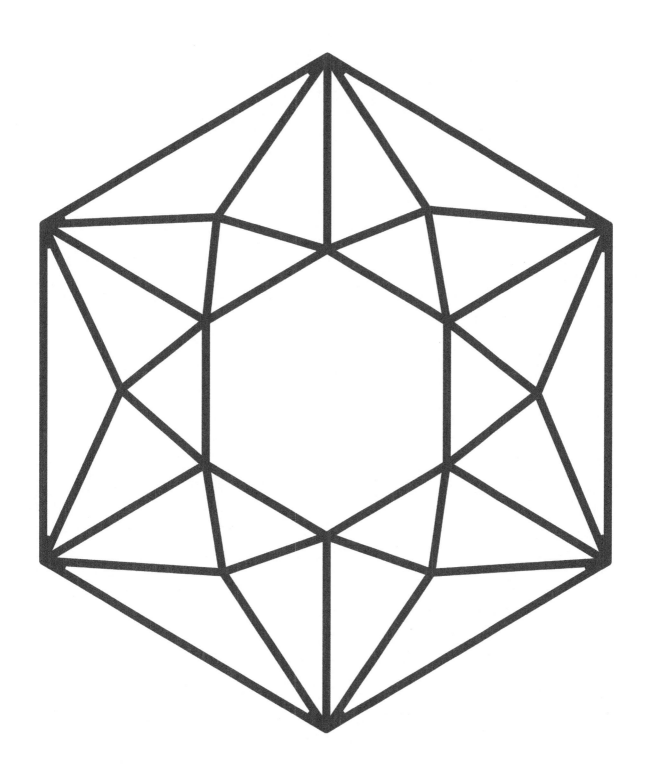

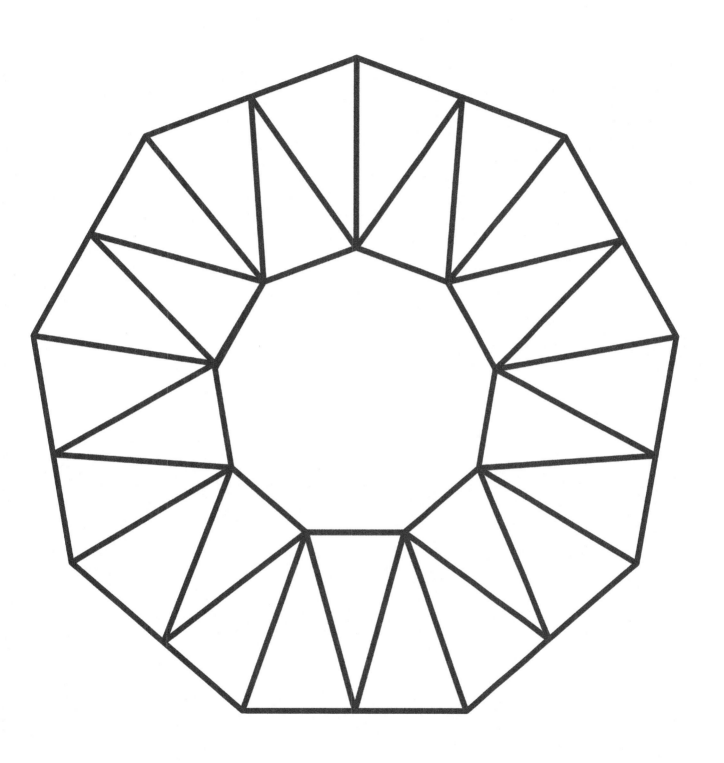

This intricate design could be used as the top of a box
or as a mirror!

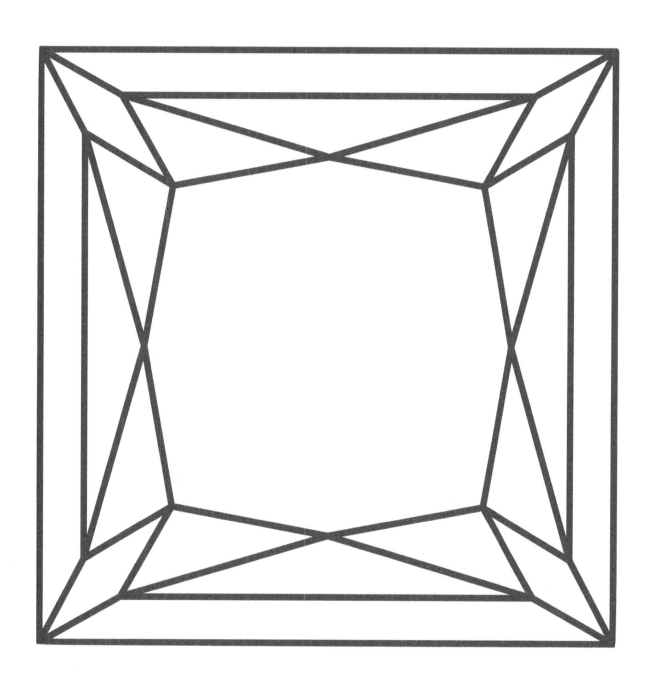

*This intricate design could be used
as the side or top of a box!*

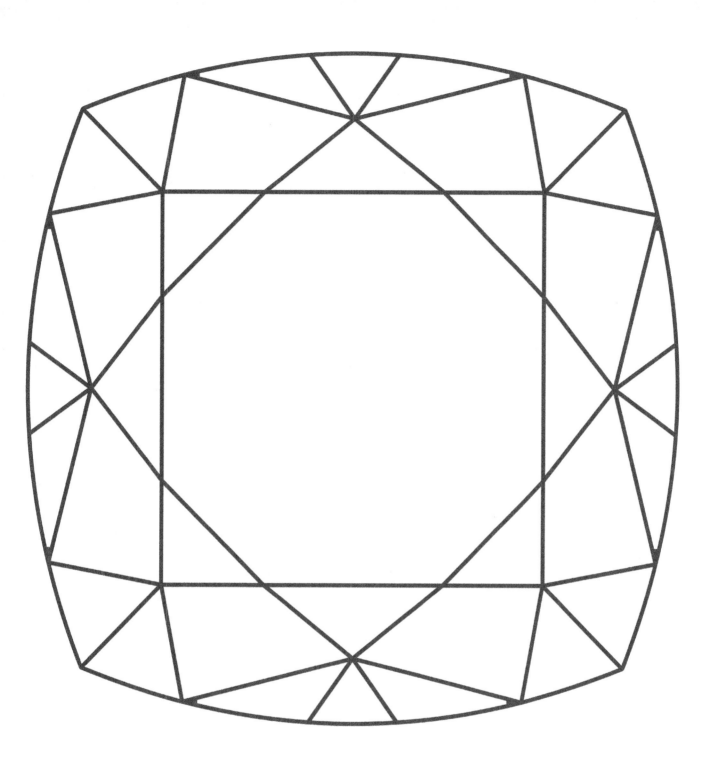

*Don't forget that all of these designs
can be reimagined as picture frames or mirrors!*

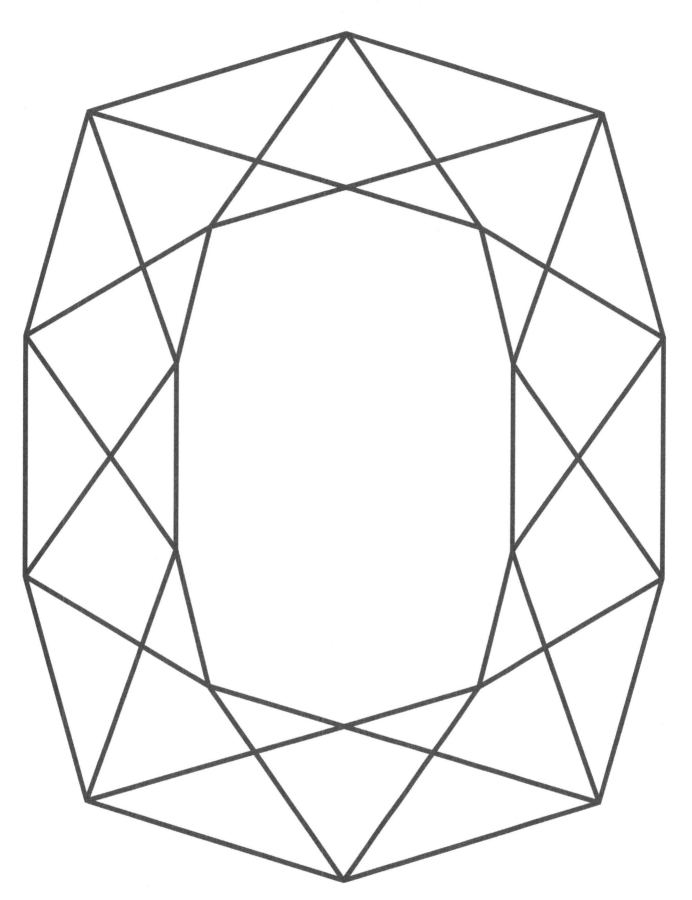

*Don't forget that all of these designs
can be reimagined as picture frames or mirrors!*

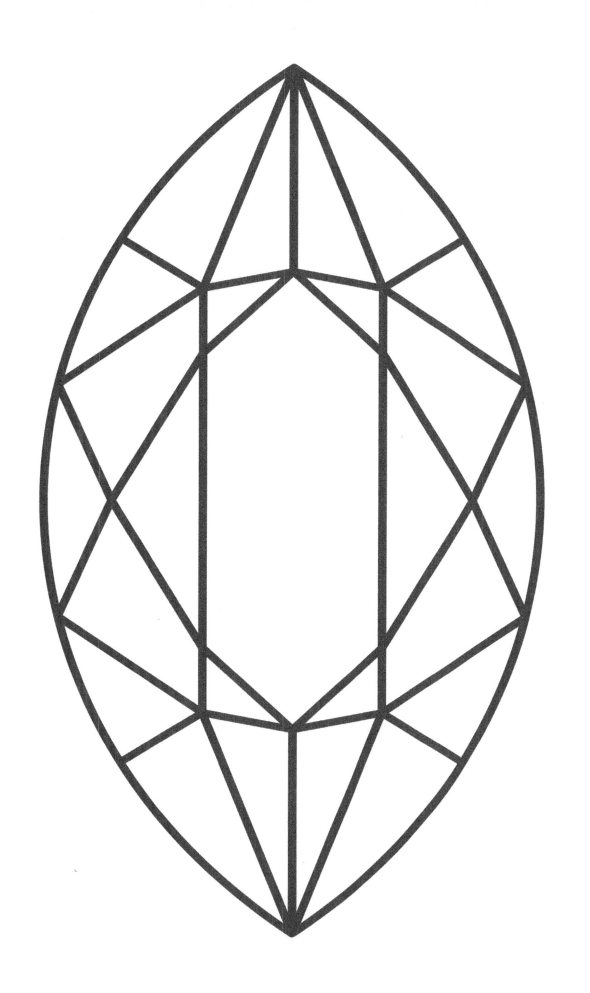

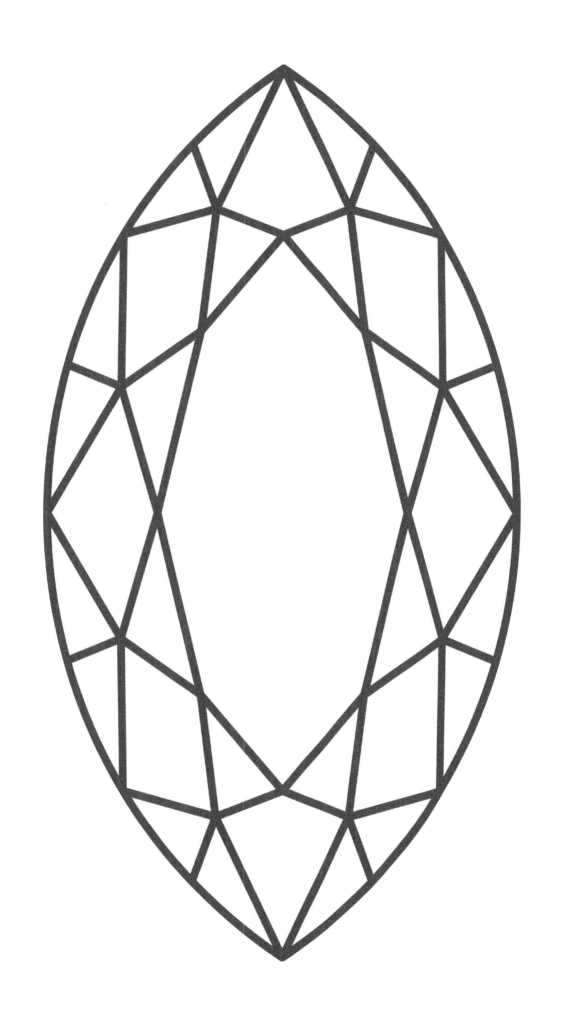

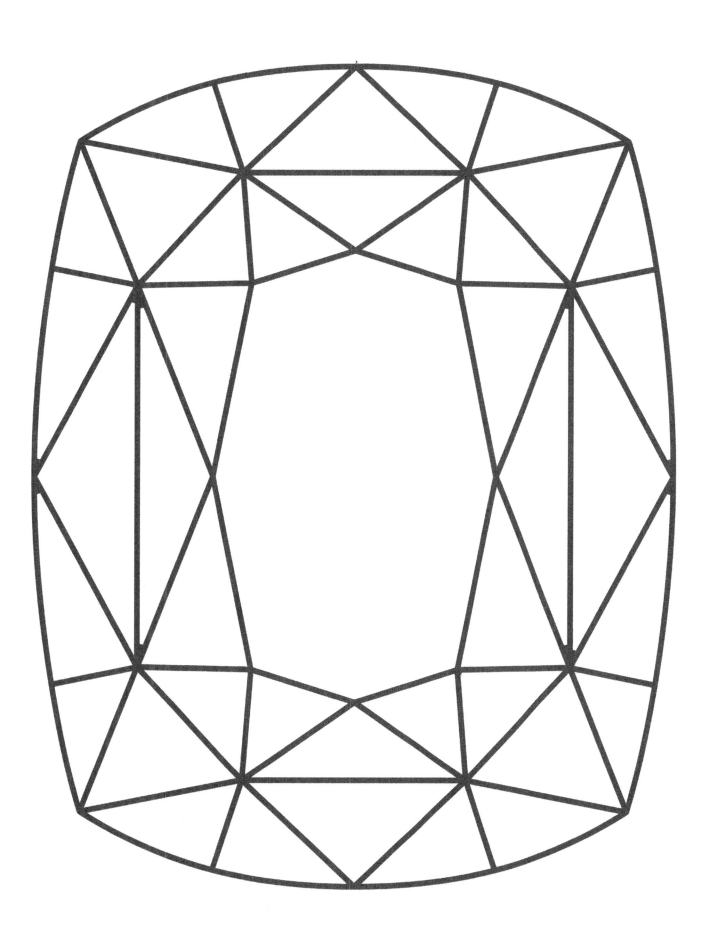

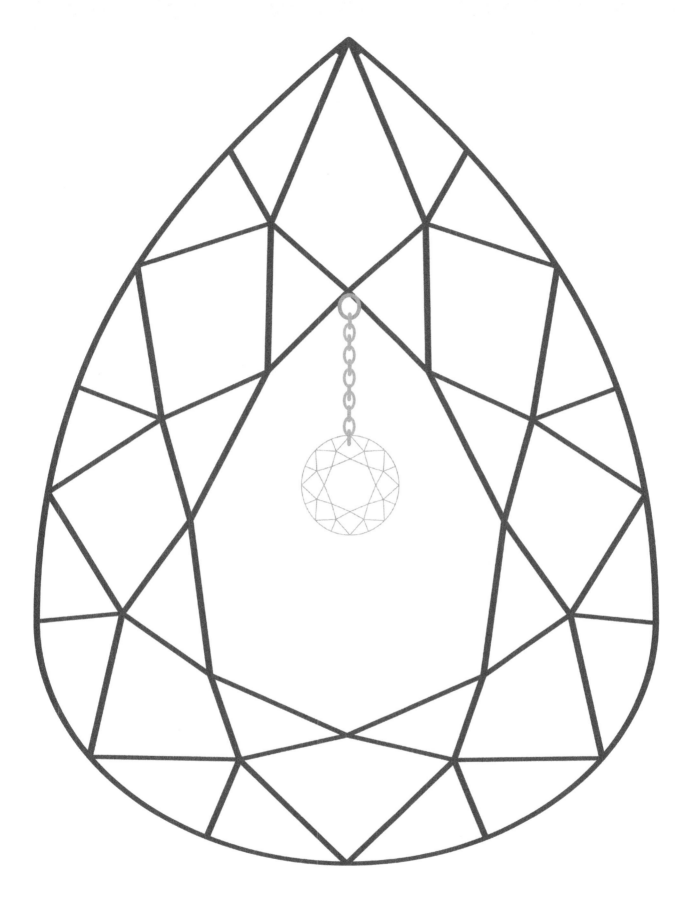

The drop style could be created without the center piece,
and then you can add a lovely crystal to hang from inside.

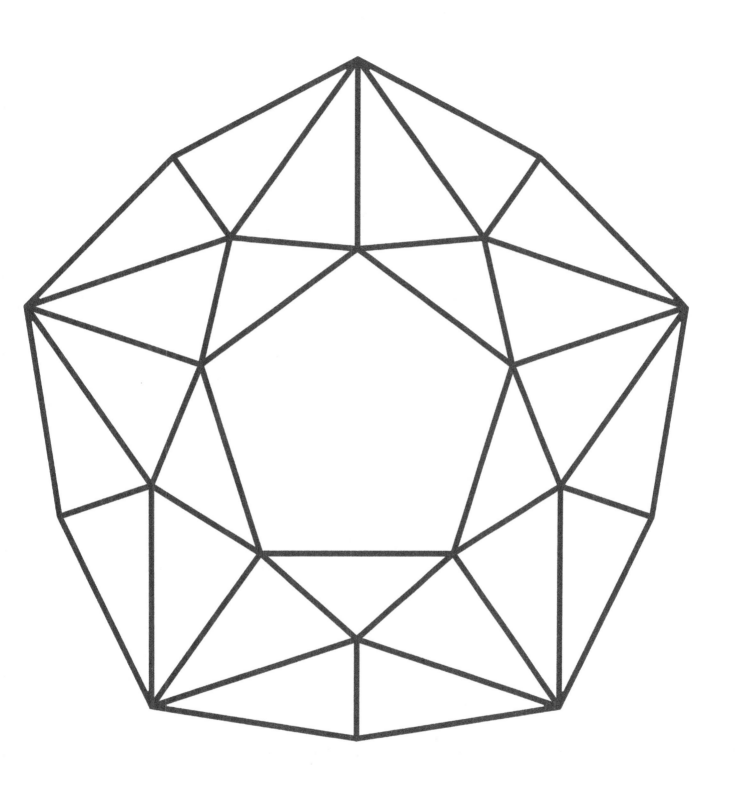

These circular-ish gems would also make a perfect mirror!

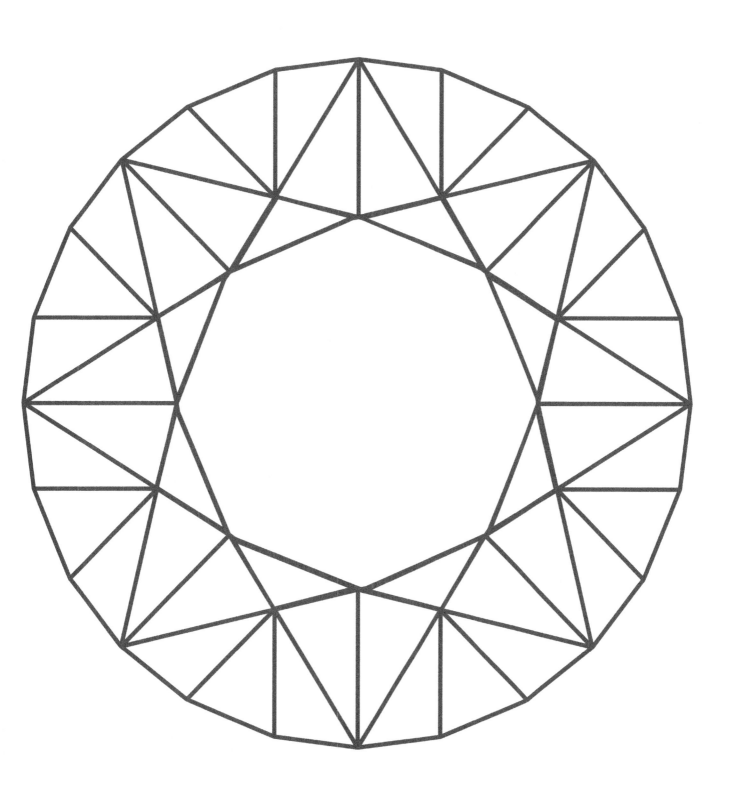

These circular gems would also make a perfect mirror!

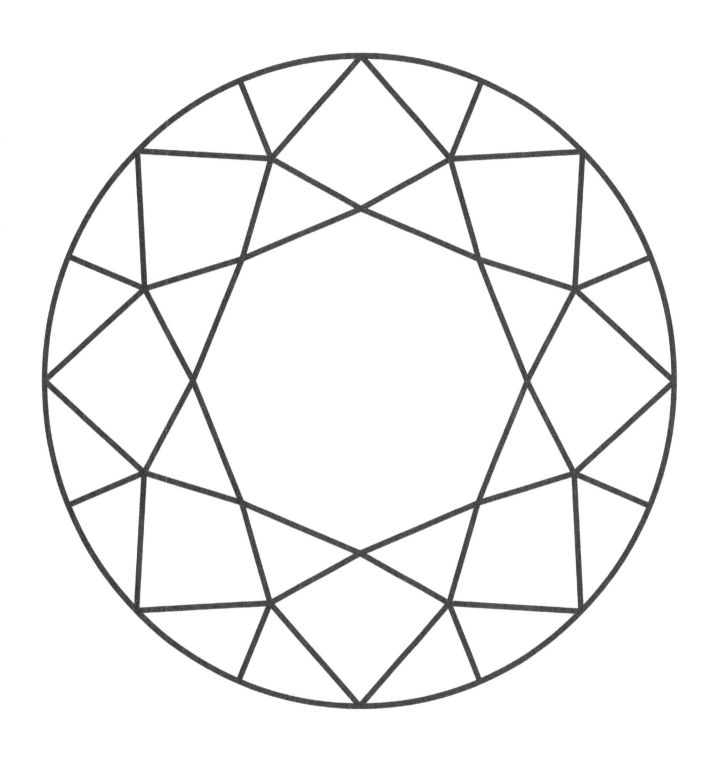

These circular gems would also make a perfect mirror!

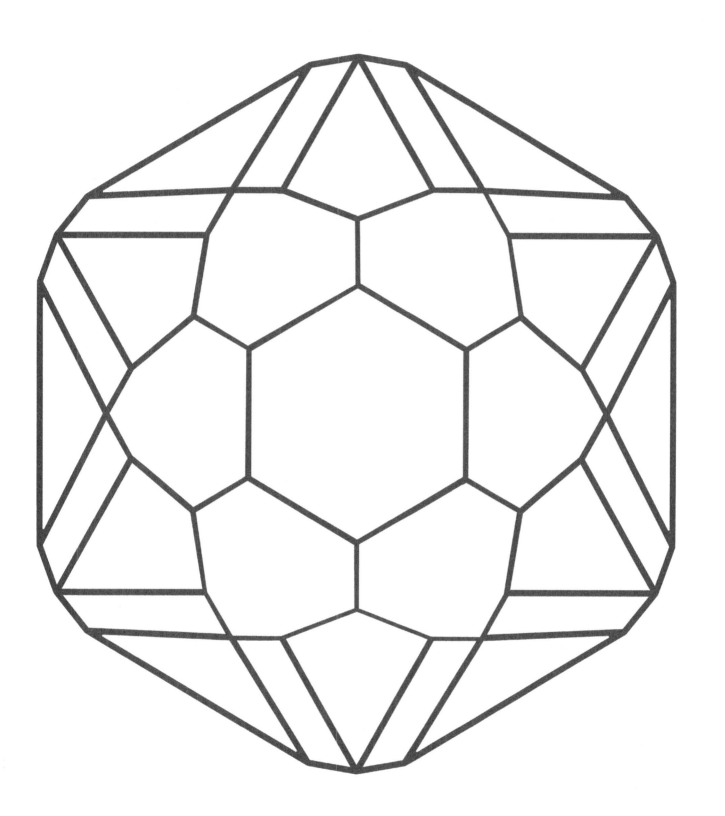

*Don't forget that all of these designs
can be reimagined as picture frames or mirrors!*

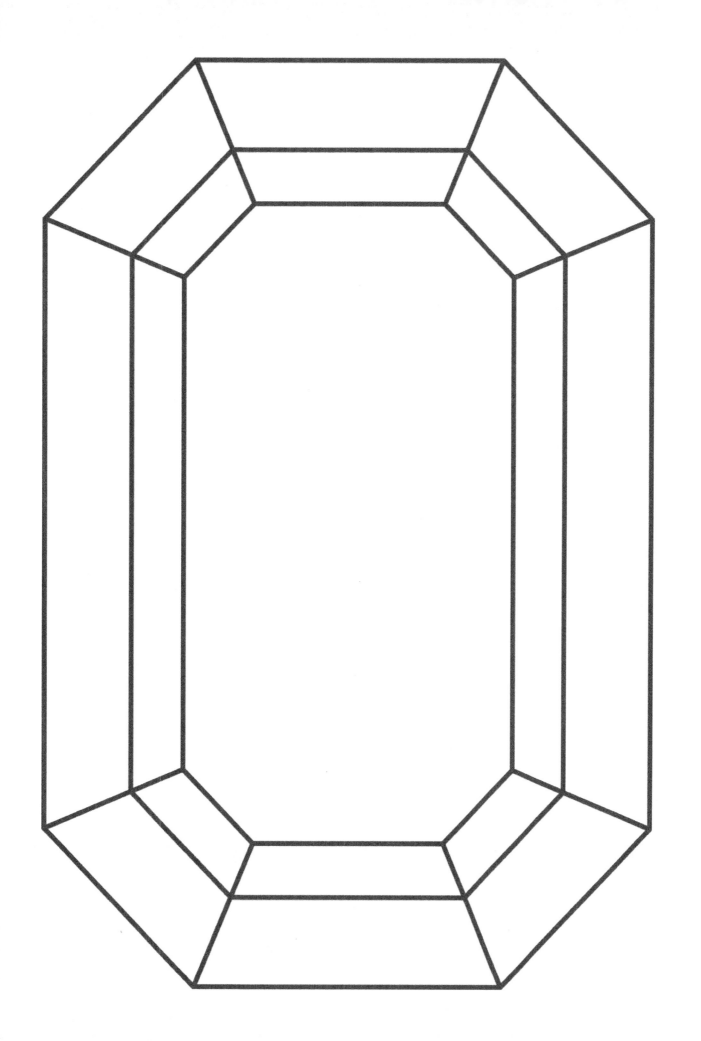

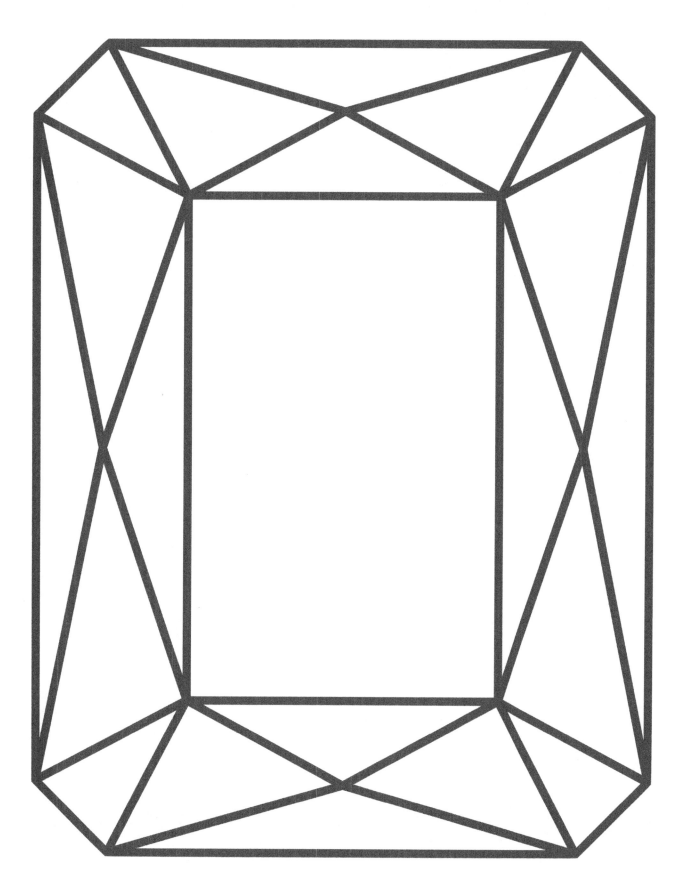

***Don't forget that all of these designs
can be reimagined as picture frames or mirrors!***

*Don't forget that all of these designs
can be reimagined as picture frames or mirrors!*

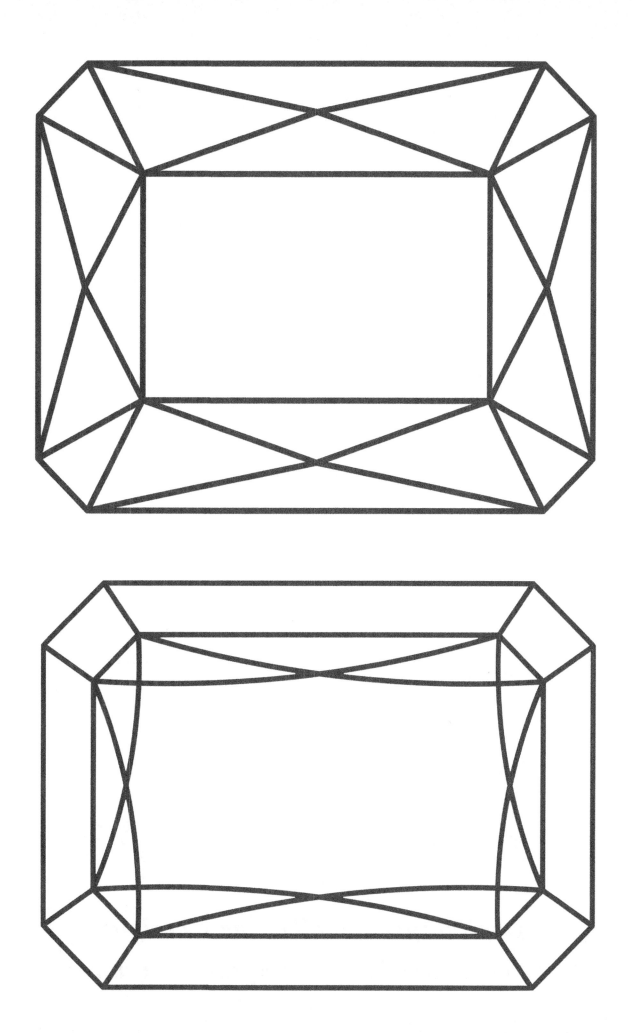

*Don't forget that all of these designs
can be reimagined as picture frames or mirrors!*

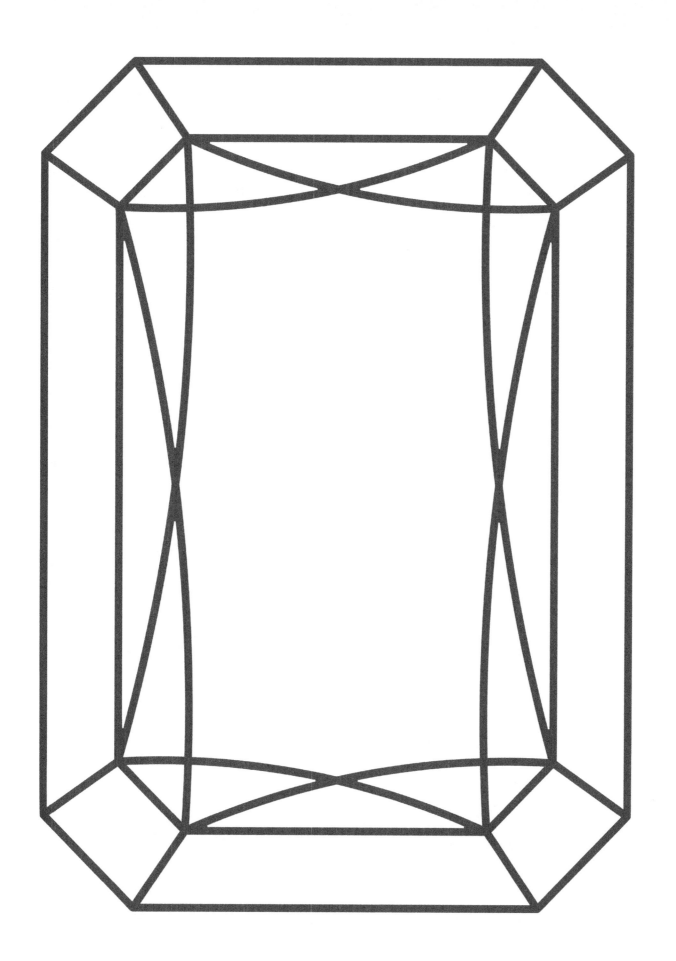

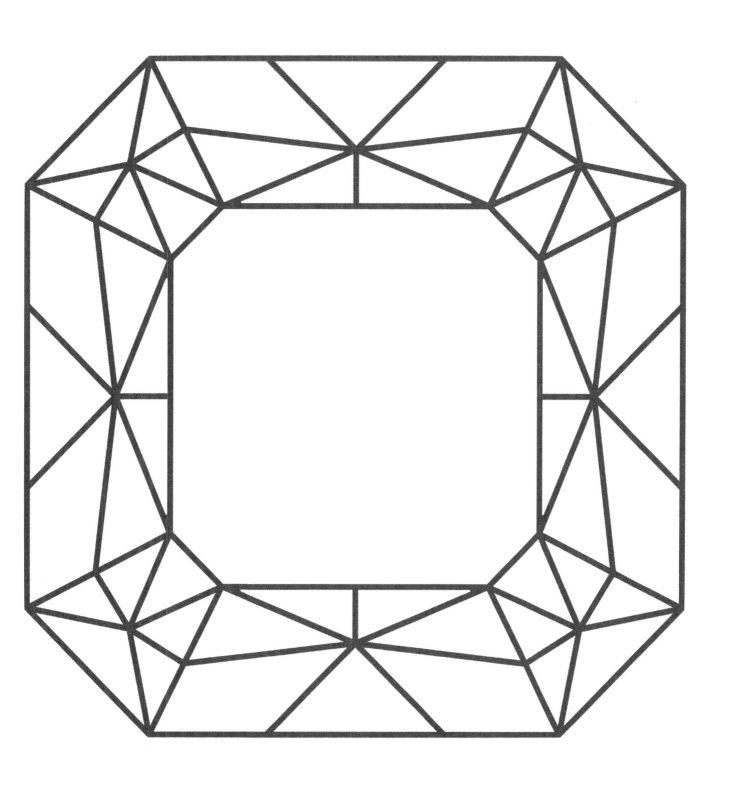

*Don't forget that all of these designs
can be reimagined as picture frames or mirrors!*

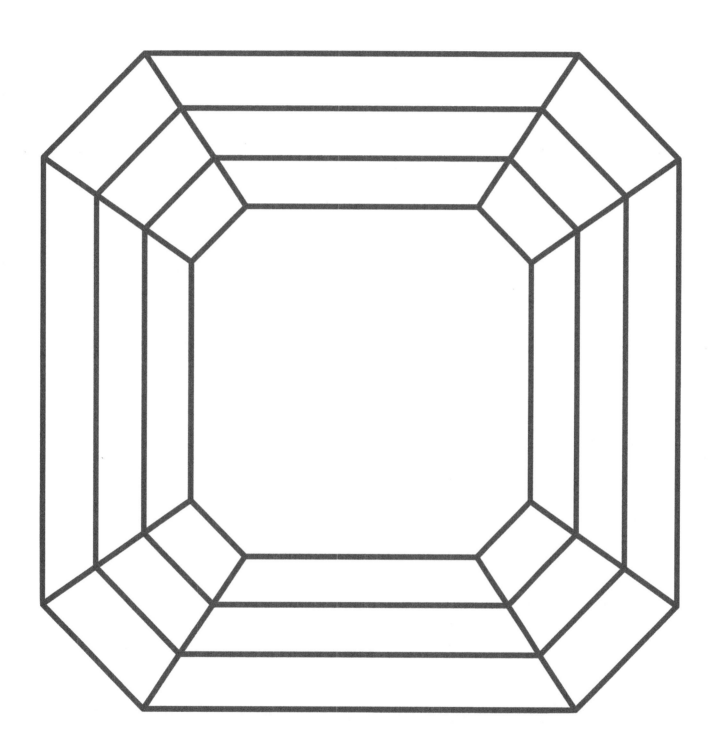

*Don't forget that all of these designs
can be reimagined as picture frames or mirrors!*

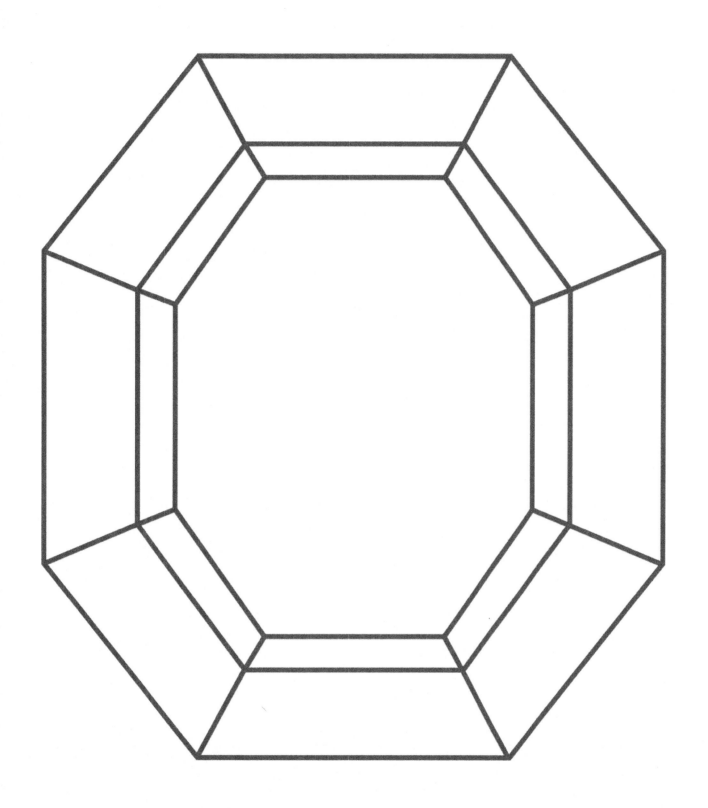

*Don't forget that all of these designs
can be reimagined as picture frames or mirrors!*

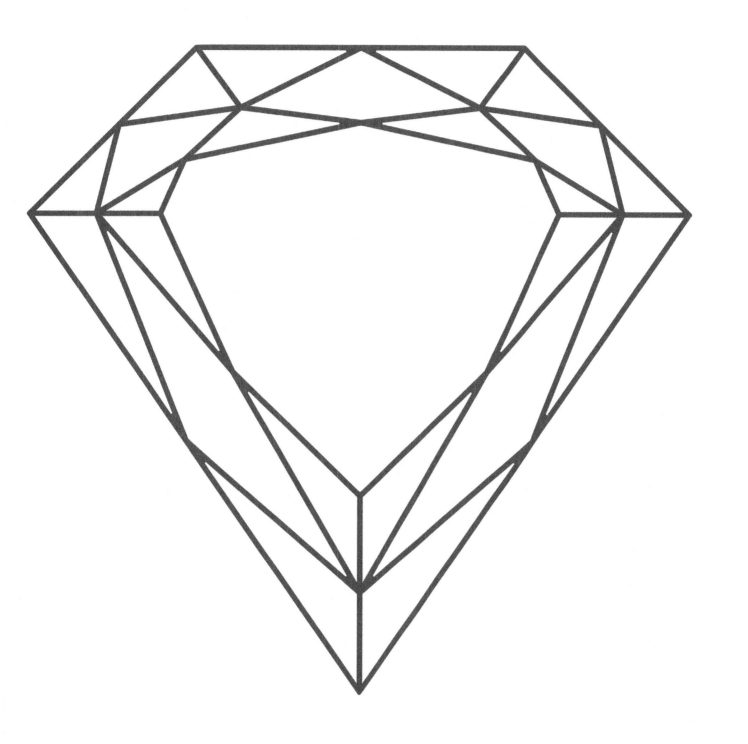

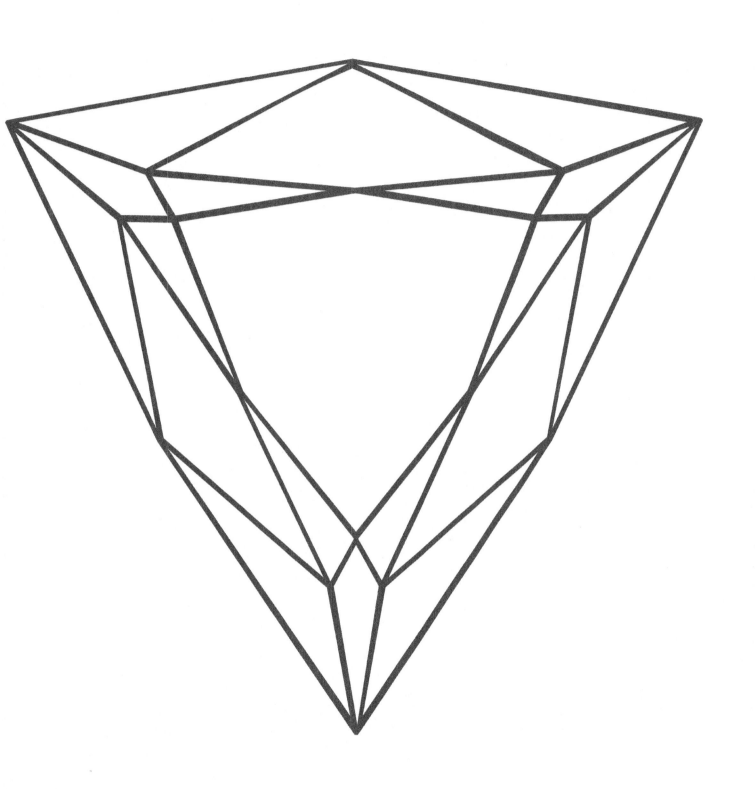

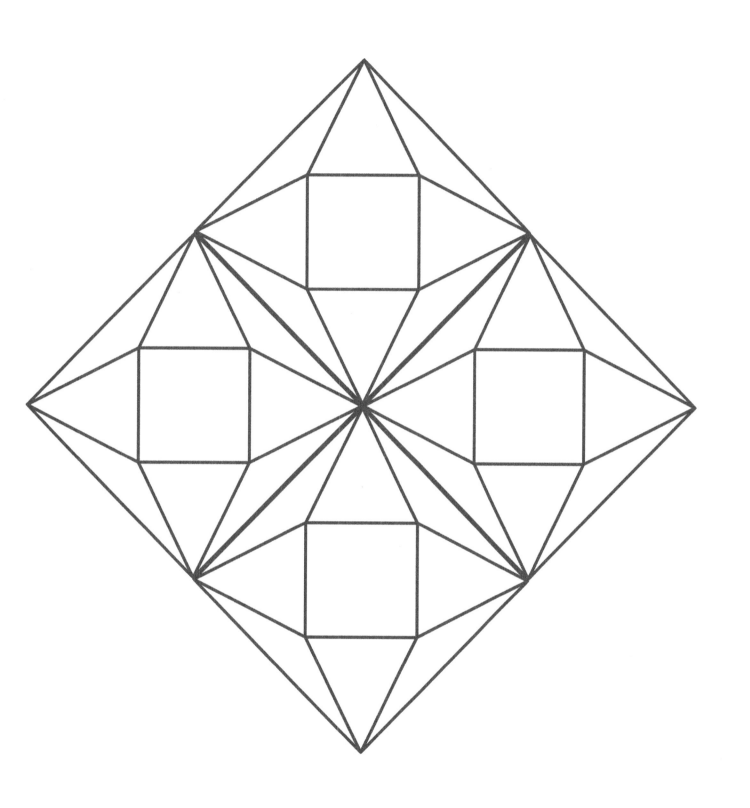

This intricate design could be used as the side or top of a box!

Made in the USA
Monee, IL
15 November 2024

70213763R00037